ANCIENT CIVILIZATIONS

THE
MESOPOTAMIANS
CONQUERORS OF THE MIDDLE EAST

by
KATHERINE REECE

Rourke
Publishing LLC
Vero Beach, Florida 32964

www.rourkepublishing.com

PHOTO CREDITS:
Courtesy Charles Reasoner: pages 9, 13, 40; Courtesy www.freestockphotos.com: pages 10, 18, 24, 27, 29, 30, 35, 38, 40; Courtesy Hirmer Verlag: cover, page 25; Courtesy Rohm Padilla: pages 7, 14, 16, 25, 36; Courtesy The Shoyen Collection, Oslo and London, ms3049, ms2192, ms2781: pages 14, 17; Courtesy Tim Alexander: page 26; Courtesy United States Department of Agriculture: pages 19, 22; Courtesy Vivianna Padilla: page 23; Courtesy Wildsmith Gallery: page 34

DESIGN AND LAYOUT: ROHM PADILLA

Library of Congress Cataloging-in-Publication Data

Reece, Katherine E., 1955-
    The Mesopotamians : conquerors of the Middle East / Katherine Reece.
        p. cm. -- (Ancient civilizations)
    Includes bibliographical references and index.
    ISBN 1-59515-237-7 (hardcover)
    1. Iraq--Civilization--To 634--Juvenile literature. I. Title. II.
Series: Reece, Katherine E., 1955-   Ancient civilizations.
    DS69.5.R44 2004
    935--dc22

                        2004012013

TITLE PAGE IMAGE
A modern re-creation of the Great Gate of Ancient Babylon, Iraq.

TABLE OF CONTENTS

INTRODUCTION

When you go shopping, wash your face, write a letter, plan an event, or even eat a meal, consider how these daily activities came to exist. Who first settled in communities, planned city streets, controlled water to grow crops, provided for fresh drinking water, or set up a calendar for planning events today, tomorrow, or next month? We take these activities for granted, but who was responsible for the very first time they happened?

A young girl in traditional clothing stands in front of domed architecture that has been used since ancient times.

Mesopotamian commoner, court official,
and noblemen in traditional dress

To find these **origins**, we look to ancient civilizations,
where a combination of necessity and environmental
conditions caused people to develop and adapt. **Mesopotamia**
(MEHS uh puh TAY MEE uh) is a region where the earliest
civilization developed.

CHAPTER 1:

WHO WERE THE MESOPOTAMIANS?

Mesopotamia is a diverse area approximately 300 miles (483 km) wide and 150 miles (242 km) long that includes present-day **Syria**, Southeast **Turkey**, and most of **Iraq**. The region is about the size of Pennsylvania in the United States today. Mesopotamia is a Greek word meaning "the land between two rivers," because the heart of the region lies between the **Tigris** and the **Euphrates** rivers. Today the Euphrates is approximately 1,740 miles (2,800 km) long, and the Tigris flows for 1,180 miles (1,890 km). These two rivers begin in eastern Turkey, flow together in southeast Iraq, and finally empty into the **Persian Gulf**. In ancient times the rivers did not **converge**, but flowed separately to the sea. The seasonal flooding of these two rivers played a major role in how ancient civilizations developed.

Mesopotamia has been called the "**Cradle of Civilization**," since scientists believe the earliest civilizations developed in Mesopotamia. A civilization is defined by a surplus of food, a division of labor, organized government and religion, and written records. A community emerges through shared beliefs and customs, and trade develops between local regions and distant lands.

As early as 5000 **B.C.E.**, there was evidence of villages existing throughout Mesopotamia. The plains of the rivers south of modern Baghdad were called the lands of **Sumer** and **Akkad** in 3000 B.C.E. Sumer was most of the southern part, and Akkad was the area located where the Tigris and Euphrates are close to each other near Baghdad today. By 1700 B.C.E., both regions were called **Babylonia** and the northern part of Mesopotamia was known as Assyria.

Map showing the area known as Mesopotamia, "the land between two rivers," and some of the ancient city locations

CHAPTER II

SUMERIANS AND THE FIRST CIVILIZATION

A group of **nomadic** people arrived about 3500 B.C.E. to an area of rich and fertile soils deposited after the Tigris and Euphrates flooded each year. Because they settled in Sumer, they were known as Sumerians.

Ancient Mesopotamian weather was most likely similar to the hot, dry climate today. Average daily summer temperatures were likely 109° F (43° C), but could climb as high as 136° F (58° C)! Dust storms were common in the long, hot summer months. Cooler winter days of 52° F (11° C) gave people more comfort, but temperatures could range from freezing to 84° F (29° C). Less than 10 inches (25 cm) of annual rainfall made these flat, low-lying plains an unlikely spot for the beginning of civilization. Yet, this region became a rich food-growing area known as "**The Fertile Crescent.**"

Reed huts in modern Iraq are similar to ones lived in by ancient Mesopotamians. In front of the huts are two river boats that are used for travel and for shipping goods up and down rivers.

Sumerian farmers lived in a sun-baked wilderness with rich soil deposits, but too little rain to farm. The secret for growing crops was to control the flooding rivers. To bring water to their fields, farmers dug ditches that eventually led to building **levees** and **irrigation** canals. No longer were Sumerians dependent upon nature and the seasons for their crops. They now controlled their environment and extended the growing seasons. As nomads, they had constantly searched for food. Now they could settle in one area and build cities.

(Above) Mesopotamians used long poles called sweeps to irrigate their fields. The pole was weighted on one end and made it easier to lift a large amount of water from the river. The water was poured into reservoirs that fed canal systems (left).

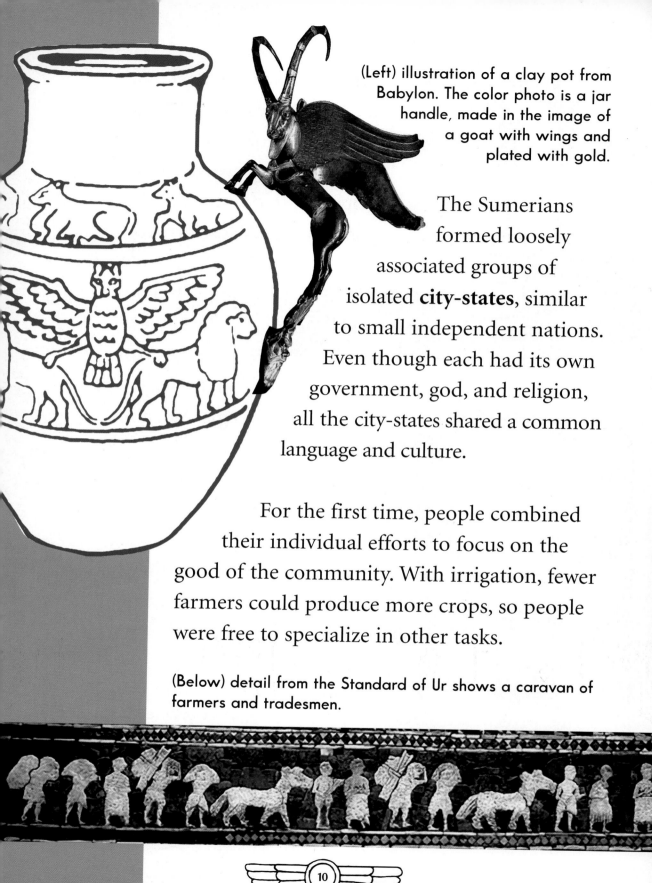

(Left) illustration of a clay pot from Babylon. The color photo is a jar handle, made in the image of a goat with wings and plated with gold.

The Sumerians formed loosely associated groups of isolated **city-states**, similar to small independent nations. Even though each had its own government, god, and religion, all the city-states shared a common language and culture.

For the first time, people combined their individual efforts to focus on the good of the community. With irrigation, fewer farmers could produce more crops, so people were free to specialize in other tasks.

(Below) detail from the Standard of Ur shows a caravan of farmers and tradesmen.

Tradesmen were needed to survey and map the land. Craftsmen became skilled in making tools and pottery. Shipbuilders made boats to use on the canals, rivers, and open seas for trade with other regions, both near and far.

Each city-state was governed by a council of elders from the town's temple. Priests became the rulers, or **lugals**, in times of conflict between city-states. The **priest-king**, or lugal, was believed to be a living link between humans and gods. He was expected to invite and encourage the blessings of the gods. His main duties included the building and maintenance of the temples and conducting religious ceremonies. Additionally, the lugal controlled the distribution of surplus foods, led the military, administered trade, and acted as judge in disputes between people.

Palace at Babylon, Iraq. The arch shows the complex brickwork of the city.

Illustration of a high priest and a king in traditional dress

The Sumerian belief that the lugal had a divine right to rule over other city-states justified their wars. Once harmony returned, the lugal continued his rule and passed it down to his sons. The world's first **monarchy** developed, in which Sumerians thought their monarch was divine and worthy of worship.

The names of the king and god of the temple were inscribed on bronze figures and placed in the foundation of temples as an offering. The figure pictured is carrying building materials in a basket.

Head of a sphinx statue carved in the likeness of a king. These giant statues were placed in pairs at the entrances of temples or important buildings.

Sumerian houses were built from available raw materials such as reeds from the river banks, mud, and clay, which were formed into bricks and dried in the sun. When stacked on top of each other, the bricks provided a thick layer of adobe that protected the family from the hot summer days and cold winter nights. Sumerians tried to waterproof these buildings by painting them. The first **mosaics** were created by using different colors to make patterns similar to woven mats and textiles. Their one- or two-story houses were built around a central courtyard. The father, mother, children, and close relatives all lived in the same house.

Illustration showing the framework of a reed hut. Mats would be laid on top for the roof.

Discovery of the wheel led to the invention of the potter's wheel.

OTHER USES OF THE WHEEL

The wheel was important in transportation, but had other uses. As a potter's wheel, it turned out beautiful clay vessels both for decoration and everyday use. Potters specialized in making all types of vessels not only for their own people, but also for trade with other regions.

Math problems involving circles, carved on clay, possibly from a royal Babylonian library, from around the 17th century B.C.E.

Sumerians are believed to have invented the wheel, and soon wagons and chariots replaced wooden sleds. Farmers transported more crops and produce because oxen pulled heavy loads in wagons. Pulleys made it easier to draw water from wells.

The invention of writing is credited to the Sumerians. They first drew simple pictures or **pictograms** to represent a word or idea. Since paper did not exist, symbols were pressed into soft, damp clay tablets using a triangular-shaped reed called a **stylus**. Then the tablets were left in the sun to dry. Pictograms were difficult to make in the clay. Soon the images were reduced to simple wedge-shaped lines or characters called **cuneiform**.

Sumerian writing emerged from necessity and marked the dawn of the information revolution. With trade, the Sumerians needed a method to keep records. Farmers had to keep **accounts** of their crops and livestock. People now could send messages to faraway lands without traveling. Knowledge could be passed from **generation** to generation. The oldest written story on Earth comes to us from ancient Sumeria. Known as The Epic of **Gilgamesh**, it tells of the adventures of the historical King of Uruk between 2750 and 2500 B.C.E.

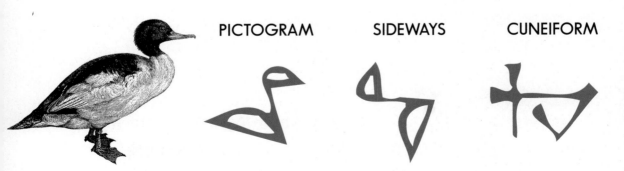

PICTOGRAM   SIDEWAYS   CUNEIFORM

The evolution of the word for bird from pictogram to cuneiform writing

Many of the deeds performed by Gilgamesh are similar to those performed by other legendary figures.

PART GOD AND PART HUMAN

Gilgamesh was a historical king who lived in 2700 B.C.E. in the city of Uruk in Babylonia. Known as the greatest king who existed, many stories and myths were written about him. Two-thirds god and one-third human, Gilgamesh was thought to possess superhuman strength and abilities. Gilgamesh built the great city of Uruk with high walls of brick. Stories of his exploits are carved on a stone of lapis lazuli at the base of the city's gates.

(Left) a mathematical problem computing the area of a triangle. The cuneiform script is etched on a circular stone. (Below) Babylonian calendar with cuneiform on a black stone from 1100-800 B.C.E. It has a handle on the right side formed like a crouching lion.

Farmers and tradesmen needed a way to plan for the future. Calendars were invented based on the cycles of the moon and twelve months. Time was measured in a circle of 360 degrees and formed the basis for the division of an hour into seconds and minutes. Numbers had to be added, subtracted, divided, and multiplied, and a system of counting evolved. Our math and science had their earliest beginnings in Mesopotamia.

CHAPTER III:

CROPS AND ANIMALS

The rich fertile plains, the mountains, and the marshlands along the river banks in Mesopotamia provided crops, wildlife, and fish. Once the farmers in Mesopotamia learned to control the flooding waters of the Tigris and Euphrates rivers, they grew grains such as wheat and barley and harvested sesame and flax from the rich soils. Wild sheep and goats that once roamed the uplands between the Meso and Zagros mountains in Northern Mesopotamia were some of the first animals to be **domesticated.** Shepherds moved their herds from pasture to pasture, fattening them on the plentiful grains. Finally, an abundance of fish and wildlife could be found in the marshes surrounding the river banks.

Wild goats were domesticated and used as a food source. Garlic was one of a variety of foods that grew in Mesopotamia.

Leeks and grapes are still a common part of the Arabic diet. Palm trees supplied dates for food.

The earliest recorded use of flax comes from Southern Mesopotamia, where it was used as long ago as 5000 B.C.E. Not only was its seed a food source, but flax was also used in making linen cloth for clothing. With a high **tensile strength**, the linen fibers could be used in products such as twine, fishing nets, and laces.

A variety of fruits and vegetables gave the Sumerians a well-balanced diet. They grew pomegranates, grapes, figs, chickpeas, lentils, beans, turnips, leeks, cucumbers, watercress, lettuces, onions, and garlic. Wild date palms that grew near the marshes were domesticated and organized into orchards.

LARGER THAN MODERN CATTLE

Bull aurochs were much bigger than cows and had horns that pointed forward rather than sweeping out to the side. Cave paintings tell us that auroch bulls were mostly black, some with a saddle patch of a lighter color, while cows and calves were red in color.

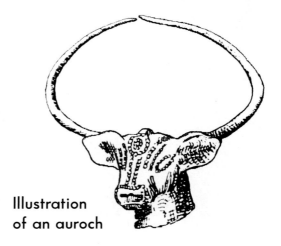

Illustration of an auroch

Aurochs would have been even larger than the bulls pictured here.

Sheep and goats grazed on the desert scrub that surrounded the well-watered fields. While sheep were first domesticated for their hides and milk, later their **fleece** became more important since it could be woven into wool. **Wild boars** were also tamed and became another food source. **Aurochs**, which were the ancestors of cattle, were used to plow fields and move heavy loads.

Pictograms show that other animals such as dogs, lions, eagles, camels, and deer were common in Mesopotamia.

CHAPTER IV

MESOPOTAMIAN CLOTHING

The Sumerians used their natural resources such as sheep's wool and flax to make their clothing. Using flax for linen, the fabric was constructed to suit the season in which it was worn. For summer, the cloth was thin, but a coarser and thicker fabric was necessary for cooler winter months. Linen was soft, but also stable and long-lasting. The more it was worn and washed, the softer and stronger it became. Linen could be **dyed** without the color fading over time.

(Left) illustration of a common Mesopotamian man in traditional clothing. (Background) the texture of woven flax would soften over time.

Illustration of wild flax

FLAX

Flax fiber is harvested and left to break down naturally. The long fibers were separated and used to make linens.

A Sumerian man might be bare-chested in the warmer months. He wore a skirt-like garment tied at the waist, and his face would be either bearded or shaven. Women's gowns covered them from their shoulders to their ankles. In draping the gown, the right arm and shoulder would be left uncovered. The women wore their hair long, but it was neatly braided and wrapped around their heads. During celebrations, women sometimes adorned themselves with headdresses. A queen's headdress might have elaborate coils of gold ribbon and wreaths of gold animals and leaves. Ladies of the court wore more modest **beech** leaf headdresses.

Jewelry was in great demand by both men and women. Wealthy Sumerians wore bracelets made of gold and silver. Gold animals and plants on a background of lapis-lazuli beads were a sign of great wealth. Necklaces were set with precious stones such as lapis lazuli, topaz, and carnelian traded from the Indus Valley. Lapis lazuli was a stone prized by the Mesopotamians and was found not only in their jewelry, but also in headdresses, clothing, and as eyes set in statues.

LAPIS LAZULI

The name of this beautiful stone comes from the Latin word "lapis," which means stone, and the Arab word "azul," which means blue. Azul was loved by ancient civilizations such as Mesopotamia.

(Above) lapis stones that have been shaped and are ready to be made into jewelry

A modern necklace made of lapis and silver. Lapis was a prized stone of the wealthy.

CHAPTER V

ARTS, CRAFTS, AND TEMPLES AS PART OF EVERYDAY LIFE

Temple walls were decorated with the stories of those who had them built.

Much can be learned about a culture from the art produced during its existence. Scenes of daily life or religious rituals may be incised, painted, or carved on articles and buildings. These pictures tell us about the wars, agriculture, beliefs, and traditions of the people. The type of material used indicates an available local resource or that a trade route was necessary to bring it from a great distance.

Cylinder seals were used to "sign" messages and to provide marks of ownership. They were necessary for recordkeeping, correspondence, and trade. Normally less than 2 inches (5 cm) long, they were often **incised** with ritual scenes, tales of the gods, or images of everyday life such as plows, nails, boats, or carts. Some were even used as jewelry.

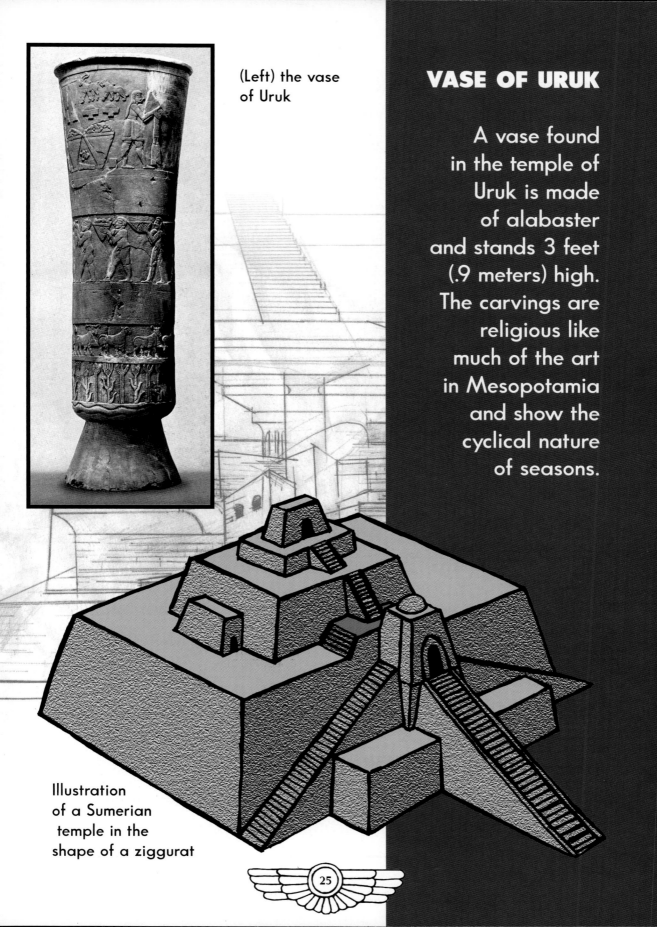

(Left) the vase of Uruk

VASE OF URUK

A vase found in the temple of Uruk is made of alabaster and stands 3 feet (.9 meters) high. The carvings are religious like much of the art in Mesopotamia and show the cyclical nature of seasons.

Illustration of a Sumerian temple in the shape of a ziggurat

Sumerians built large temples called **ziggurats** for their gods. These structures symbolized mountains, which were the source of water and represented the whole Earth. Built with thousands of mud-bricks in three to seven levels, the ziggurat's walls were often multicolored mosaics. They painted the exposed ends of baked clay or pressed stone into the clay to produce patterns. A road, often wide enough for a horse-drawn chariot, circled the structure and allowed people to ascend with their offerings and prayers.

A multicolored mosaic of a lion from ancient Babylon

Local temples housed a local god or goddess whose image was displayed in a **niche** behind the altar. The sculpture was crafted in human form and treated as a living being. **Statuettes** made of stone, copper, gypsum, or terracotta stood in front of the altar with large eyes staring forward and their hands clasped in prayer. Some of these images were made of diorite, a hard stone believed to have been quarried in Oman and transported through the Persian Gulf.

CHAPTER VI:

CENTER OF TRADE

A wall carving showing farmers and livestock. At left is a walled city with wheeled chariots pulled by aurochs (large cattle). A date palm tree towers above the wall and the people pay a tribute to the ruler of the city in the center of the carving.

Mesopotamia soon became the center of the ancient world's trade. With its fertile soils and irrigation, large surpluses of food were available. Canals provided waterways for shipments of grains and crops. The mountains to the west had timber, limestone, gold, silver, and copper. Flax from the river valleys and wool from sheep could be traded between the city-states for items they did not have.

The canals and rivers were busy with trade between city-states within Mesopotamia. Wooden boats traveled easily through the canals and rivers that emptied into the Persian Gulf and led to civilizations outside the region. By 3000 B.C.E., trade routes stretched across the entire Middle East. From the Iranian **plateau** of the present day, they crossed through Iraq and into southern Turkey. The relatively small size of the Persian Gulf made it easy to move goods between Mesopotamia and the Nile Valley in Egypt, another rapidly developing region.

Along these trade routes, outposts were built for the collection of goods to be traded from that region. A mountain outpost could send copper ore, semiprecious stones, timber, hides, and animals downstream into Mesopotamia. These centers flourished as the demand for these resources increased in the city-states of Mesopotamia.

A variety of exotic resources were shipped in and out of Mesopotamia by way of the Persian Gulf. Tolls were collected for shipped goods at outposts along the way.

CHAPTER VII:

WAR AND CONQUEST

Archers attack a city from a chariot while more archers defend from the top of the wall.

Mesopotamia's history was marked with numerous wars and invasions. Unprotected by natural terrain, the diverse city-states were open to attack. Busy cities attracted more **rural** dwellers, and the growth in population put a strain on housing. Water from irrigation **leached** salts from the soils and reduced fertility. The Euphrates River slowly shifted to the west, leaving whole cities stranded in the desert. As areas lost access to water, people were forced to move to more favorable locations.

The need for water and land led to power struggles between cities. Walls were built around the city-states for protection from neighbors who needed the same resources. The larger, more powerful city-states **engulfed** smaller ones. When at war, more men were needed for the military, and labor was taken from the more productive trades. This constant internal battling weakened Sumer and made it **vulnerable** to attack.

SARGON I

Sargon I was the earliest king to maintain a permanent army and appoint members of his royal court as governors of conquered states. His policy of expansion brought the city-states under one god. Sargon I ruled his empire for more than 50 years, and his reign was so well organized that it survived for 60 years under his successors.

In 2300 B.C.E., a group of people who lived in the northern parts of Mesopotamia attacked the city of Sumer. Led by **Sargon I** of Akkad, they conquered the Sumerian city-states and united

A winged sphinx (human-headed lion) with head carved in the image of Sargon II, a later Mesopotamian king with the same name.

them to create the first **empire** in history. Within his life-time, Sargon's empire stretched from Mesopotamia to the east in what is present-day Iran, west to the Mediterranean Sea, and north to Asia Minor (Turkey).

These **Semites** spoke a language similar to modern-day Hebrew or Arabic and replaced Sumerians as the most powerful inhabitants in Mesopotamia under the rule of Sargon I. Known as **Akkadians** after the name of their capital city of Akkad in the north, they kept their native language, but adopted the Sumerian system of cuneiform for their written language. They also kept the Sumerian government, literature, and law, while adding improvements of their own.

Around 2125, the Sumerians in the city of Ur, located on the Euphrates, reunited the surrounding city-states in a period of harmony as Sargon's empire began to lose power. Dependence on water contributed to Ur's collapse as the Euphrates River shifted its course, and rivalry between the city-states increased. Eventually they fell to **Amorites**, who migrated south from present-day Syria in 1800 B.C.E. The Amorites had been uprooted by **droughts** many times in their own homelands, but their semi-nomadic life came to an end in the fertile plains of Mesopotamia.

The Amorites constructed their own city-states. Babylon was ruled by King **Hammurabi,** who conquered the Sumerian city-states and once again united them under one empire called the Kingdom of Babylonia. Lasting from 1792 to 1750 B.C.E., King Hammurabi's reign was called the "Golden Age of Babylon" because of his many **reforms.**

King Hammurabi was devoted to protecting his frontiers and promoting **prosperity** in his empire. He personally supervised navigation, irrigation, agriculture, and tax collection, and he built many temples and buildings. He gave his personal attention to such details as the cleaning of the irrigation canals and added an extra month to the Sumerian calendar. The people of his kingdom were also united under one religion and one god.

Hammurabi was a wise lawgiver and is remembered for the Code of Hammurabi. Inscribed on stone **stele,** his code was placed in temples throughout his realm. Hammurabi required that people of his empire be responsible for their actions, so offenses and specific penalties were outlined. These laws provided a uniform and consistent system of justice for all aspects of daily life. Hammurabi's Code of Law survived him and served as a guideline for future rulers.

HAMMURABI'S CODE OF LAW

Babylonians introduced the idea that laws protected commoners and peasants, as well as noblemen. Hammurabi's Code made the state responsible for enforcing the law. The punishment for breaking a law was based on "an eye for an eye and a tooth for a tooth." For example, if a house in Babylonia collapsed and killed the owner, the builder of the house was to be put to death.

(Left) Hammurabi's code was inscribed in stone.

CHAPTER VIII:

BELIEFS AND GODS

Clay figurines of the goddess Ishtar from Mesopotamia. Many ancient cultures show their deities in this pose, which is known among archaeologists as "The Ishtar Pose." Ishtar was known as Innana in Sumeria. Rituals and stories about her are thought to be based on the cycles of the moon.

Mesopotamians were **polytheistic**, which means the people believed in many gods. Mesopotamians believed the gods created the world and all people in it. They were super-humans with all of mankind created to serve them. Their gods and goddesses ate, drank, looked, and acted like humans. Although the gods were believed to be **immortal**, they married and had children.

One god or goddess governed each city-state. If captured, a city-state was forced to accept the new god of its conqueror. There were additional gods or goddesses for each trade, such as potters, scribes, or farmers. Individuals depended on their own personal god who would help them, much like a guardian angel.

Gods were also believed to have emotions like humans. When some natural disaster such as a flood occurred, people thought that one of the gods was angry. Their gods lived in the skies or heavens and ruled over humans on Earth through natural forces.

A winged deity anoints a king with sap. The deity holds a pine cone and uses sap taken from a palm tree.

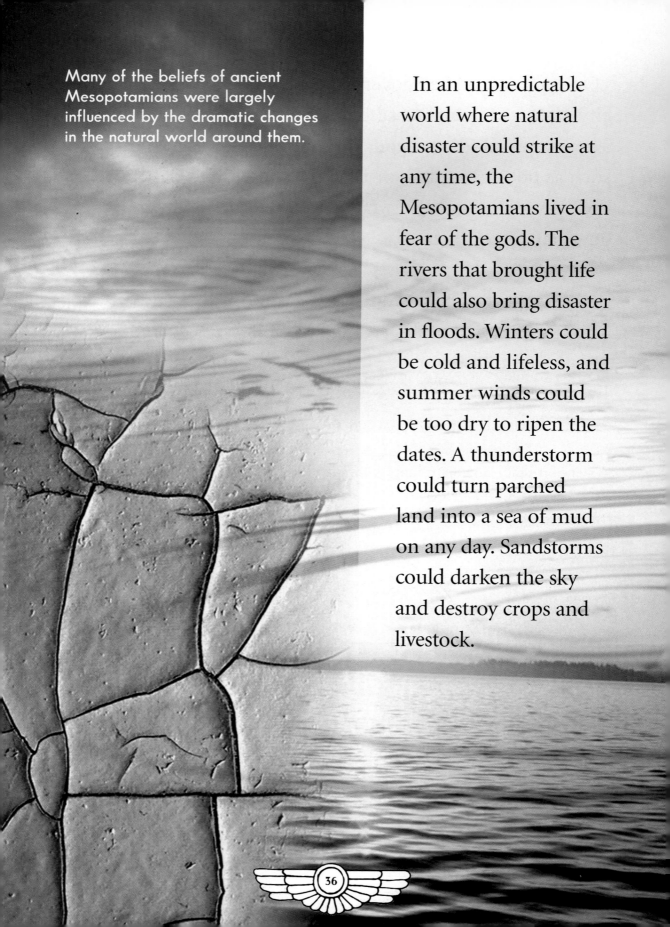

Many of the beliefs of ancient Mesopotamians were largely influenced by the dramatic changes in the natural world around them.

In an unpredictable world where natural disaster could strike at any time, the Mesopotamians lived in fear of the gods. The rivers that brought life could also bring disaster in floods. Winters could be cold and lifeless, and summer winds could be too dry to ripen the dates. A thunderstorm could turn parched land into a sea of mud on any day. Sandstorms could darken the sky and destroy crops and livestock.

Mesopotamians believed good and evil were results of their god's will. They looked to the gods for favor and protection, and believed all their needs would be met if they treated the gods well. The gods were given daily offerings of food and drink, lodging, and gifts of art.

Many goods such as dates and eggs were offered as daily sacrifices for special treatment by the gods.

MENU FOR THE GODS

Here is a daily menu for the god Anu at Uruk:
- 12 vessels of wine
- 2 vessels of milk
- 108 vessels of beer
- 243 loaves of bread
- 29 bushels of dates
- 21 rams
- 2 bulls
- 1 bullock
- 8 lambs
- 60 birds
- 3 cranes
- 7 ducks
- 4 wild boars
- 3 ostrich eggs
- 3 duck eggs

Everyone owned a statuette in which it was believed that the person was physically represented in the sculpture. Only priests were allowed to go inside the temple, so the common people needed representation before their city's god. People would place statuettes at altars to worship the gods constantly, so that they were free to go about their daily activities without neglecting the gods.

Mesopotamians regarded their gods with love and admiration, but also with submission and fear. For everyone, obedience to divine orders was the greatest of qualities, and service to the gods was a duty that could not be avoided or taken lightly. Sumerians believed that gods communicated to people through the priests and rulers. Priests handled the **rituals** in the temples, but it was every person's duty to observe all the rules and do good deeds while on Earth, so they would be looked upon with favor by the gods.

Statuettes were believed to represent worshippers and would be left in the temple to pray constantly for the owner.

CHAPTER IX:
DEATH AND AFTERLIFE

As a reward for good deeds, the gods gave protection, good health, comfort in distress, long life, and happiness. But for all their good deeds on Earth, humans could never expect to have eternal life. Death for ancient Mesopotamians sent them on a journey to the underworld called the Land of No. Kings and common people alike were stripped of their clothing and possessions and left hungry and thirsty to roam for all time.

Burial rites and preparation of the dead for the journey to the Land of No was extensive and planned with great care. The body was washed, clothed in linens, and then laid on its side with a bowl of water close to the mouth. The dead were then laid in small tombs that were lined and covered with mud bricks. Along with food and sandals, as many treasured belongings as the family could afford were placed in the tomb for the trip to the underworld.

Many modern beliefs were inspired by ancient rituals, such as burial in a tomb. Here is a tomb in modern Syria.

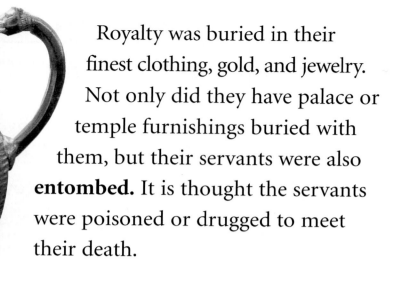

Royalty was buried in their finest clothing, gold, and jewelry. Not only did they have palace or temple furnishings buried with them, but their servants were also **entombed.** It is thought the servants were poisoned or drugged to meet their death.

(Above) valuables would be buried with their wealthy owners.

The mourning period for the dead was a very public display and continued for seven days. Professional mourners were hired to grieve for the dead. Vessels filled with food and water were not only buried with the deceased, but monthly offerings of food and prayer were continued for years so the spirit of the dead would not be hungry and return for food.

Religious items such as this eye-idol have been found at some sites. These objects may have been offered as a prayer to a specific god.

CHAPTER X:
THE PEOPLE TODAY

Most of Mesopotamia has become a part of a nation known as Iraq. As in ancient times, desert covers most of the land. Fields that were once productive have returned to barren mud flats. Dust storms alternate with heavy rains, but water is still scarce. As far as one can see to the north and south, there is a vast wasteland of sand. With a shortage of land for agriculture and lack of industry, economic progress has been slow.

Instead of a fertile crescent for agriculture, the most valuable resource of the land today is oil and its export. The long history of invasions and conquests has continued into current times. Wars have damaged trade routes and the country's oil reserves.

Modern Iraqis at the walls of Nineveh in Mosul, Iraq

Most of the 24 million people in Iraq live in cities such as the capital, Baghdad, Basra in the south, and Mosul in the north. Cars, trucks, and buses travel between tall buildings; museums house art; students attend schools and universities; and people work making carpets, textiles, cement, and tobacco products. In the urban areas, the upper and middle classes wear western styles of clothing just like you would find in Europe or North America. The laborers wear more traditional clothing. Men still wear long cotton gowns with jackets, and women wear long, concealing gowns with a **burka**, or scarf, that covers much of their heads.

This popular Muslim pilgrimage site in Najaf, Iraq, shows that traditional influences are still strong on modern cultures.

Life outside the cities continues much the same as it has for centuries. Nomads move through the deserts and mountains herding camels, goats, and sheep. To this day they depend upon the animals for all their necessities. Their tents are made of goat or camel hair. They use the meat, milk, and cheese as food and their clothing is made from animal hides or hair.

Rural people follow ways rooted in the past. They raise barley, wheat, dates, olives, and other fruits to feed their families. Their clothing with long, flowing robes and **turbans** on their heads is similar to their ancestors. Their mud and adobe homes are huddled in groups of fifty or more to form small villages.

Iraq illustrates a modern urban civilization alongside rural settlements with people whose customs and culture are the same as centuries past. Indeed, there are few other countries in the world where the past is more strangely alive.

A TIMELINE OF THE HISTORY
OF MESOPOTAMIA

5000 B.C.E.   Earliest evidence of mud-brick villages in Mesopotamia.

3500 B.C.E.   Sumerians settle on the banks of the Euphrates. Cuneiform writing on clay tablets. Ziggurat temples built. City governments known as city-states.

3000 B.C.E.   Councils of elders give way to kingships, which evolve into monarchies.

2750 B.C.E.   Gilgamesh, hero of Sumerian legends, reigns as king of Uruk.

2500 B.C.E.   Epic tale of Gilgamesh is written.

2300 B.C.E.   Akkadians led by Sargon I attack and conquer Sumerian city-states.

2125 B.C.E.   Sumerians around the city of Ur on the Euphrates reunite and gain independence.

1800 B.C.E.   Amorites from the Syrian desert migrate to Mesopotamia and construct their own city-states. Hammurabi ascends Babylonian throne.

1792-1750 B.C.E.   Hammurabi brings most of Mesopotamia to include Sumer and Akkad under his control. Golden Age of Babylonia. Hammurabi introduces law code.

GLOSSARY

Akkad: City of northern Mesopotamia near modern-day Baghdad.

Account: A record of items bought and sold or traded.

Akkadians: A group of Semitic people who conquered the Sumerians around 2300 B.C.E.

Amorites: Various Semitic peoples living in Mesopotamia, Syria, and Palestine during the third and second millennia B.C.E.

Aurochs: Extinct, large, long-horned wild oxen that are the ancestors of domestic cattle.

Babylonia: An ancient Mesopotamian empire that extended throughout the Fertile Crescent in the 1700s B.C.E.

B.C.E.: "Before the Common Era," or before the year "1." This term is similar to using B.C., which refers to time before the birth of Christ.

Beech: A hardwood tree with smooth gray bark and small edible nuts.

Burka: A scarf worn by women in Iraq and other Muslim countries, which hides the face.

City-state: Sumerians organized themselves into groups of competing city-states. Each city-state consisted of the city, the surrounding mud brick wall and farmland. In the center of the city-state was the ziggurat.

Converge: To come together.

Cradle of Civilization: Mesopotamia is known as the "cradle of civilization" because the world's first civilization began there.

Cuneiform: The system of writing created by the ancient Sumerians. They used "wedge-shaped characters" called cuneiform.

Cylinder Seals: Seals first used in Mesopotamia to indicate a message on a clay tablet was genuine or to indicate ownership of a possession.

Domesticate: To bring an animal or plant to live in close contact with and to the advantage of humans.

Droughts: Extended periods of dry weather with little or no rain.

Dye: To give a new and permanent color to the fabric by making it a part of the fabric.

Empire: A collection of kingdoms under one powerful ruler.

Engulf: To flow over and enclose.

Entomb: To bury.

Fertile Crescent: A region of western Asia that is shaped like a quarter moon and covers present-day Iraq, Syria, Lebanon, and Israel.

Fleece: The coat of wool covering a wool-bearing animal such as a sheep.

Generation: The average length of time between the birth of parents and that of their children.

Gilgamesh: An important mythical hero to the Sumerians who was strong, intelligent, and an invincible fighter.

Hammurabi, King of Babylon: The king of Babylon from 1792 to 1750 B.C.E.

Incise: To cut or carve figures, letters, or pictures into a surface.

Immortal: Exempt from death; living forever.

Iraq: An Arab country at the head of the Persian Gulf in southwestern Asia.

Irrigation: Bringing water to an area by artificial means.

Leach: To remove nutrients from the soil as a result of water drawing the nutrient out of the soil.

Levees: Raised areas of earth used to hold back floodwaters.

Lugal: The name for the priest-king or ruler of a city-state in Mesopotamia.

Mesopotamia: An area located between the Tigris and Euphrates rivers. The word is in origin a Greek name (mesos "middle" and potamos "river," so "land between the rivers.")

Monarchy: An undivided rule or absolute rule by a single person.

Mosaic: A surface decoration made by inlaying small pieces of different colored material to form pictures or patterns.

Nomadic: People who have no fixed place to live and move from place to place within a specific area when the season changes or they are in search of food.

Niche: A recess or indentation in a wall made especially for a statue.

Origin: The point at which something begins.

Persian Gulf: A section of the Arabian Sea between Southwest Iran and Arabia.

Pictogram: Earliest forms of writing used by the Sumerians.

Plateau: A large area of land with a level surface that rises high above the land on at least one side.

Polytheistic: The belief or worship of more than one god.

Priest-king: In Mesopotamia, the priest of the city-state's temple became the ruler with many powers and absolute authority.

Prosperity: The condition of being successful or thriving; related to production, distribution, and consumption of goods and services.

Reform: An improved form or condition.

Ritual: A formal act or series of acts that is based on religion or social customs.

Rural: Country people or life.

Sargon I: King of Akkad who conquered the surrounding Sumerian city-states to create the first empire.

Semite: A member of any number of people of ancient southwestern Asia including Akkadians, Phoenicians, Hebrews, and Arabs. These people spoke a Semitic language such as Hebrew or Arabic.

Statuette: A small statue or representation of a person made by sculpturing.

Stele: A stone slab or pillar carved, marked, or engraved with something to be remembered.

Stylus: A wedge-shaped writing instrument made out of reed.

Sumer: The earliest civilization, which began around 3500 B.C.E. It was made up of a group of ancient city-states in southern Mesopotamia.

Syria: Ancient region of Southwest Asia, which bordered on the Mediterranean Sea and covered modern-day Syria, Lebanon, Israel, and Jordan.

Tigris and Euphrates: The two rivers that begin in the Taurus Mountains and flow to the Persian Gulf.

Tensile strength: The greatest stress a material can bear without tearing apart.

Turban: A headdress worn by Muslim males and made of a cap with a long cloth wrapped around it.

Turkey: A country in western Asia and south-eastern Europe between the Mediterranean and Black seas.

Vulnerable: Open to attack or damage.

Wild Boar: A wild hog from which most tamed pigs came.

Ziggurat: An ancient Mesopotamian temple tower built in stages with outside staircases and a shrine at the top.

Books of Interest

Lost Civilizations. *Sumer: Cities of Eden*. Time Life Books, 1993.

Lost Civilizations. *Mesopotamia: The Mighty Kings*. Time Life Books, 1997.

Honour, Hugh and Fleming, John. *The Visual Arts: A History*. Fourth Edition, 1995.

Web Sites

www.dl.ket.org/humanities/connections/class/ancient/index.htm

www.dl.ket.org/humanities/connections/class/ancient/mesopreligion.htm

www.coconino.edu/apetersen/_ART201/mesopot.htm

home.echo-on.net/~smithda/hammurabi.html

www.sron.nl/~jheise/akkadian/mesopotamia.html

www.mrdowling.com/603mesopotamia.html

grassroots.brunnet.net/fundyhs/ancient_times/mesopotamia.htm

INDEX

Katherine E. Reece is a native of Georgia, where she grew up in a small town located in the foothills of the Blue Ridge Mountains. She has traveled throughout the United States, Europe, Australia, and New Zealand. Katherine completed her Bachelor of Fine Arts with an emphasis in studio art at the University of Colorado in Boulder, Colorado, where she now resides. Her extensive studies in art history gives her an appreciation for all that can be learned about the culture, beliefs, and traditions of ancient civilizations from the architecture, artifacts, and recordings that have been preserved through the centuries.